Windforest

Windforest
Spirit Brooding on Brooding Spirit

ELLEN FREMEDON

CONTINUUM
New York   ✧   London

2000

The Continuum International Publishing Group Inc
370 Lexington Avenue, New York, NY 10017

The Continuum International Publishing Group Ltd
Wellington House, 125 Strand, London WC2R 0BB

Printed in the United States of America

Library of Congress Cataloging-in-Publication Data

Fremedon, Ellen.
    Windforest : spirit brooding on brooding spirit /
Ellen Fremedon.
        p. cm.
    ISBN 0-8264-1277-7 (alk. paper)
    1. Meditation. 2. Life.   I. Title.
BL627 .F74 2000
291.4'32—dc21
                                                        00-034066

For Michael Armstrong:
invictus manet

. . . darkness covered the abyss, while a mighty wind swept over
the waters.   (Genesis)

There are times when the light vanishes
behind darkening clouds;
then comes the wind, sweeping them away,
and brightness spreads from the north.   (Job)

He said to me, 'Prophesy to the wind,
prophesy, man, and say to it,
These are the words of the Lord God:
Come, O wind, come from every quarter
and breathe into these slain,
that they may come to life.'   (Ezekiel)

The wind blows wherever it pleases;
you hear its sound,
but you cannot tell where it comes from or where it is going.
That is how it is with all who are born of the Spirit.   (John)

CONTENTS

Preface   13
Rainforests   17
Breath   21
Fresh Air   25
Sharing Breath   29
The Whole *Rainforest   33*
Animals, Plants, and Wind   37
Thinking the Wind   41
The Winds of the Windforest   45
Celebrating the Winds   49
The United Nation of Winds   53
Turmoil and Taming   57
A Reconsideration of Prejudice   63
Spiritus Mundi   67
Taking in the Breath of the Windforest   71
In a Zen Temple   73
In the Temple, Failing   77
The Temple, Winddrift   81
In the Temple, in the Wind   87
Another Changing   91
The Misleading Lightness of Elation   95
Cultivation   101
A Parting Word   107

Windforest

PREFACE

*M*editation, like love, may be either religious or not. Like love, it may take many forms; and like love, all the forms have at least one thing in common. All the kinds of love lift the lovers out of the usual boundaries of themselves and at least for a while make them belong to an endearing someone, or to a cherished elsewhere, or to a treasured something, and make the lovers willing to let go of a self-possession they usually cling to as if it were their real selves, so that they can reach out to belong to what is beloved. To love, to care for, someone or somewhere or something, is not a longing to possess, which sometimes masquerades as love, but a dispossession that leaves one less self-contained, wiser through more belonging, and less alone.

Meditation is any way of turning the mind and imagination either inward or outward in order to dispossess oneself of self-restriction and see something— or everything—differently. An insight is a momentary meditation because it is a seeing differently. An insight may permanently alter your way of seeing something (or everything), or it may prove untrue and fade away; but the new seeing it gives you may possibly change your life. An education is a sustained meditation designed to help you see a vast set of truths you had not seen before, and to value them appropriately and to grasp how they may be related to one another, and to you. What is more usually called meditation is similar to both: it is an extended insight, or outsight, or the two together, in which you try an unusual way of seeing that may make a wholesome difference in the way you see once the meditation ends.

The little book that follows is a guide into the Windforest as a scheme of meditation, placing you within the Windforest and leading you along some of its paths until you see how you may visit and explore it on your own.

There are really two windforests. One is this book: *Windforest*. The other is the Windforest itself, to which *Windforest* is only an introduction. Once you have finished *Windforest*, you may wish to return to it again as an aid to further meditational visits to the Windforest, but the book will no longer be necessary. You can simply give it away and return to the Windforest itself on your own, in your own ways, revisiting your favorite places or finding new ones that the book does not mention. By then you will know that you live in a true Windforest, and that it is inexhaustible, and that it is a home that you like belonging in. Once it is yours, the matrix that you have discovered is no longer in the book: the Windforest is in you, and you in it.

All this will become clear as you read *Windforest*.

Eventually, the Windforest may become closer than your own backyard or favorite chair, and you may slip in and out of it as you please at any time, in any place, under any conditions. The same is true of *Windforest*, and the reason why it is small is so that it may be as close as you wish it to be while you make your way into the Windforest that is your own. Once you are there, you may possibly decide never to leave, never to let your imagination forget that you are there, even when you concentrate on something quite different. Eventually, you will see that *Windforest* is useful only because it is part of the Windforest itself, and a very tiny part even if it was the door through which you entered. *Windforest* only invites you into the real Windforest, and welcomes you to walk in it anywhere, anytime, and as far away from this book door as you please.

Rainforests

Rainforest is as familiar as *Windforest* is not: but to know about the rainforest is to start knowing the Windforest.

Even a nodding direct acquaintance with a rainforest is a formidable and sobering experience. Fly over a rainforest in a plane, and it looks like the earthly counterpart of a grumpy but frozen ocean. The floor below it is unreachably hidden in the depths of a wine-dark not-quite-green sea of dense rough unbroken surface that stretches as far as the horizon; no treetrunks are visible, no boughs are swaying in the breeze, no movement breaks the perfect stillness; there is no sign of the abundant life within, nor even of life in the thick crust that hides it, which is made of a matting of functioning leaves but looks no more lively than a discarded Christmas tree.

Enter a rainforest from its outer wall, and it may seem to be the decaying ruins of a once-thriving civilization of vegetational greatness, now pathlessly mingled and tangled, forebodingly dark and silent: "delicacy" is not a word that comes readily to mind. You know that you must not enter unguided, or you can be swallowed, consumed, and buried without leaving a trace.

Look at our past confrontations with rainforests, and you see monuments to former Davids who faced Goliaths without their slings. Excavating Mayan ruins in Yucatán is like trying to interview defeated insurgents who are now sequestered in hiding and afraid to speak; in Cambodia, the huge artistic stateliness of Angkor Wat belies the generations of labor required to recover it from the engulfing rainforest, and in Angkor Thom we can still see the same battle being lost again as massive trees straddle and crush temple walls, and vines creep across the huge stone faces of meditating Buddhas.

Rainforests do not look as if anyone needs to worry about whether they survive. They more easily raise the question of whether *we* will.

But we know more than we see; and one of the surprising things that we now know is that despite the impression that rainforests are devastatingly and unrelentingly encroaching glaciers and slow-moving permanent thunderstorms of vegetation, apparently destined to take over all the earth, they are in fact in serious peril.

For all their stolid formidable appearances, the world's rainforests are as mortal as we are, and are always threatened. They are permanently at the mercy, and the mercilessness, of changes in climate, lightning-struck fires, and newly transported or mutated pests. Even puny human beings, who have always lost their previous battles with the rainforests, have now ganged up on them more successfully: we have added to their troubles a huge increase in the harvesting of trees, the clearing of land for agriculture, the building of roads and factories and housing.

The life of rainforests is precarious because of powers that neither we nor they can control, and powers that we do not adequately choose to control, and even deliberate human efforts intended to make life better. We have begun to awaken to realizing that some ways of making some lives better make many more lives worse, all over a world that is, like a rainforest itself, much more fragile than it seems. In the meantime, the world's forests are disappearing at the rate of 1 percent per year, a rate that simple mathematics shows will steadily rise even if there is a slight *decrease* in the total numbers of trees felled and acres cleared annually.

Saving the rainforests is not romantic. The rainforests are to be cared for not merely because they have a beauty all their own, or because they arbor hundreds of thousands of forms of precious and often endangered life—unthinkable billions of living creatures more intricate and amazing than anything we have ever made. We should always remember that these considerations are part of the rainforests' truth, but there are also more selfish interests for us to bear in mind. We must care for the rainforests because we depend on them. Some people depend on them for their livelihood, but that is a small matter when measured against what else they can do for us. A frog found in the Ecuadorean rainforest produces a painkilling substance that is two hundred times more powerful than morphine and non-addictive; it could eventually put a dangerous drug out of clinical business and tempting access by providing far better and safer relief for intense and chronic pain. And there is more: all of us depend on rainforests for what makes our own life *possible.*

Breath

The heart beats long before the child is born. The blood circulates, the brain is drowsily awake, the muscles contract and thrust toes and elbows into the wall of the womb. But there is no breath. There is no breath in the baby because there is breath in the mother, through whom the child within shares the fruits of breath. If her breath fails, the baby's heart and brain and muscles and life will fail too. For breath is life. When the baby is born, and is severed from the mother's breath, it must have breath of its own in order to live. From now on, there must be either breath or death.

But not just any breath will do. Breath that takes in poisons can kill the breather directly. Breath that crowds out the usual air may be stifling: breathing the smoke of a burning rainforest can swiftly stop the body's life.

Carbon dioxide is abundant in normal air, and harmless to breathe—but breath that takes in *only* carbon dioxide is not enough to live on. Watch a sink fill up with a soft cloud as a piece of dry ice melts not to liquid but directly to a heavy gas that pushes out the usual air, and then put your face down into the cloud and breathe: there is no pain, no stifling, no silent poisoning, but also no nourishment. There is no free oxygen, and thus no breath of life. You will pull your face out and gasp—not just with surprise.

As we breathe, we take into our bodies everything that air is. Most of what air is made of, we cannot use. Our lungs sift out the oxygen and expel the rest. As we breathe out, we put back the carbon dioxide we took in, and the nitrogen, keeping only enough of the oxygen to sustain us. High on a mountain, the air is thin and a breathful offers less oxygen: there we gasp for more air because our bodies need just as much oxygen as they did far down below. If

the air is thin, our breathing must be thick. We pant, as
if we had been running rather than resting, and think of
going back down.

High on a mountain, the air is fresh but thin. Low
in a sealed room, the air is thicker but soon grows—
what? We say "stale," but breathing is more delicate
than eating. Old dry bread is nourishing even if un-
pleasant. The unpleasantness of air that grows steadily
stale in a sealed room is far more ominous, more like
land that grows stale from crops that eat up what nourishes them and leave less and less for the crops of next
year, until the time comes when we must move on to
fresh land in order to grow *our* nourishment. The air
in the sealed room is not becoming thinner. It is in fact
becoming thicker, like the fog in the sink. We are using
up the oxygen, and it will not be replaced.

She is using up the oxygen. So is he: all of us in the
room. When we breathe the air in, we are breathing in
more and more carbon dioxide along with less oxygen.
Not just because the proportions are changing as the
oxygen is used, but because we breathe out more carbon
dioxide than we take in. We take it in as free oxygen, but
much of what we breathe out is unfree oxygen that is of
no use to us anymore, because taking it in as the stuff of
life involves reorganizing it in our bodies. The same pro-
cess that gives us life transforms the free oxygen into car-
bon dioxide. The sink is filling up. Whether you are in
the room alone or with others, anyone who is breathing
will eventually die unless there can be fresh air.

Fresh Air

"*F*resh" air. Air with more free oxygen. Where will it come from? Open the door, break a window, knock down a wall if necessary in order to get the air we're used to, rich with oxygen, into our underfed lungs. That will save us.

But only for a while. The world itself is a sealed room. Not far beyond the place high on the mountain, the air stops altogether. There are no walls or sealed windows, but neither is there air: there is only an empty place, and unless we take oxygen with us when we go there, we die. Down below, everyone is breathing, using up the oxygen. There is no breaking out from the sealed world, and no fresh air left on some grand Outside that we can get through to. The sink is filling. What will save us? What *can* save us?

If we were alone, the billions of us all sealed in the world's room, we would all drown in carbon dioxide, and the last emerging baby would breathe in vain and only briefly.

But we are not alone. In the vast sealed room, there are rainforests.

The rainforests are breathers too. They are made up of vast societies of breathing plants that can save us, because they breathe the other way around. The trees, the vines, the bushes, the flowering plants, the grasses, all breathe in what is to them life-giving carbon dioxide and breathe out free oxygen, which is of no use to them but is indispensable to the animals that live among them. Within the rainforests there are billions of other breathers like us, large and tiny animals who use up free oxygen and breathe out carbon dioxide that is of no use to them, but indispensable to the rainforest plants.

The rainforests have the last word in this exchange: they are big enough to make more free oxygen than they spend on those who dwell within them like babies within their mothering. There is enough left over for us too.

The plants are breathing not only for themselves, but for the inside and outside animals as well. What is expelled by the plants because it is not lifegiving to them is necessary to the life of the animals. The two can breathe and live, because they have each other, each giving away what the other needs to survive.

Once upon a time, long long ago, there was no free oxygen. Our planet is the only place where free oxygen can now be found, but there was a time when there was none even here. All was changed dramatically when plants emerged: it made animals possible. Now the air has a good reserve of free oxygen, thanks to the plants; we would be able to last for a while even if the plants did not replenish the supply. But only for a while. We need the plants, even if not yet urgently. They need us too.

The rainforests give away far more free oxygen than their own animals need. But the animals within it give away far less carbon dioxide than the rainforest plants require, and the supply in the air is already very low. Plants now have to live on thin air, like animals at high altitudes, and cannot readily afford a further reduction in the carbon dioxide supply. The rainforests can't stall for time by moving to a less depleted place. Their clock is awfully slow by comparison with ours, but it is ticking their life away all the same. If a rainforest and its inhabiting animals were alone together in a sealed room, both would be doomed. Eventually, the plants would wither for lack of lifegiving carbon dioxide, and would cease to breathe out free oxygen; the animals would then die too.

It can also go the other way. The experimental Biosphere II is a miniature Earth-system: a very large, complex sealed greenhouse with its own little ocean, desert, and savannah, stocked with representative animals and plants of highly various kinds, including food-crops that were already mature when the eight human beings who had agreed to stay inside for two years entered and closed the door. All went well enough for a few months, but the free oxygen supply began to decline steadily until a third of it was gone. The animals began to die: the tropical birds perished, then all seven species of frogs. The mounting carbon dioxide levels rose to ten times normal, and killed the ocean-life; over fifteeen tons of free oxygen had to be pumped in to save the people, and the experiment. The sealed room was supposed to be self-sustaining by the combination of the mutually helpful animals and plants, but it failed. How bad is that news?

It is very serious. The world itself *is* a sealed room! It must be self-sustaining in the same way that the Biosphere II greenhouse was supposed to be. That greenhouse did not have enough plant life to satisfy the needs of the oxygen-users. In the great greenhouse that is the world, there are still enough plants, but they are being steadily diminished by thoughtless profiteering. What will save them?

Sharing Breath

*W*hat will save them is the wind.

The nearly motionless rainforests are sealed within the emptiness that surrounds the world; but despite their immobility, they are not entirely sealed in place within the world itself. The wind carries the plants' out-

breathed free oxygen over the world, right to the freshened air just outside the sealed room in which a few people are gasping in their isolation. Break a window, knock down a wall, and they suddenly receive what a rainforest has offered them from thousands of miles away—air that is fresh to them, however stale it may be for plants. The wind brings the gift of the rainforests to our lungs, unseals the room we occupy, freshens our air with life. That is why we need the rainforests. That is how we can help them. That is also why we both need the wind.

The wind does not blow only in one direction. If it only carried the freed oxygen from the rainforests to us, the rainforests would perish for lack of carbon dioxide. But as we give out the carbon dioxide that is useless to us, the wind carries it eventually to the rainforests, and the cycle begins again. Together, the two kinds of breathers give life to one another within the confines of the sealed world, because of the wind that binds us together and makes our lives mutually possible. *All living things are bound together in this way, each giving into the wind what others need. The wind is the world's bloodstream.*

A rainforest is dense with plants at every point where we can approach it. "Impenetrable" we sometimes say, and so it nearly is at its outer margins and along its riverbanks and occasional clearings, where sunlight fosters the growth of plants of all sizes, packed far more thickly than we can crowd our densest cities. And so it is, in another way, within the forest, where the trees, competing for precious sunlight, grow a crowded canopy so thick that not enough light is admitted to permit smaller plants to grow beneath it. But a rainforest is not impenetrable to the wind that brings it life.

A rainforest goes nowhere, rooted deeply into a limited part of the earth. Plants of various kinds may touch one another more directly only if they are rooted close together: the vine embraces the sapling, twining around it for support; the mosses spread along the lower tree-trunk; the branches of this tree rub in the wind against the branches of that one; the rootless orchid dangles from the reaching limbs.

But the orchid hangs from the tree in order to open itself to the sustaining air that moves to bring it nourishment. The rooted rainforests live for centuries, millenia, eons, only because the penetrating wind assists the insects in carryings their pollen into new generations. Blossoms grow fruitful because of breezes. Most plants bear blossoms that can fertilize each other through the slightest stirring of the air, but some plants are divided into males and females, and can reproduce only through a wind that can unite them despite their rooted separation. In a rainforest, life survives and thrives because of the wind. One rainforest can touch another one only through the wind. It is the wind, and the wind only, that puts us all in touch with one another.

Above the rainforest in Kauai looms the mountain Waialeale, nearly a mile high, that stops the clouds drifting on the tradewinds from the northeast and forces out the water they carry. More rain falls here than on any other place on the planet—over fifty feet per year, once almost four feet in a single twenty-four-hour day—leaving rivers and waterfalls and a vegetation that abounds with an unusual diversity of flowering plants and trees. The western part of the island is almost barren of life of any kind, since the ample gifts of the wind are all bestowed on the other side of the mountain, where the cloudbearing strength of the tradewind stops cold and the resulting rain washes the eastern lowlands until life flourishes prodigally. This is the oldest and therefore the most wind-weathered of the main Hawaiian islands; the wind and the rain it bears have had time enough to turn its barren volcanic rock into sustaining soil, and the plants arrived long ago to take advantage of it, with the help of the wind. The only indigenous mammal is a small bat. The first human beings arrived relatively recently, probably less than 1,500 years ago. They came, of course, on the wind, in sailboats, to enjoy the paradise that the wind had made.

The Whole Rainforest

*O*n a map, what we usually think of as a rainforest shows up as a large or small separate patch. The map does not tell the whole truth. These patches are not really separate, because of the wind.

The wind unites the rainforests with one another, but also unites them with all the plants that cover the earth around the rainforest patches and between them.

There is no name for the plantscape between the rainforest patches.

There are many truths that do not have a name. Truths do not need names. But we do. We notice truths with names much more easily than truths we have not yet named, and naming is a way of realizing a truth that we had not noticed before. All the plants are bound together by the wind, and they live more closely together than the eye and map can see, all of them doing what a rainforest does in a much denser and more concentrated way. They should be thought of, and named, together.

The rainforests are the megacities of the plant world, but they have much in common with the metaphorical towns, villages, and scattered farmhouses of similar plants, and the whole population should have a way of being named together. The most convenient way at the moment is to say that all together, they constitute a single united Rainforest, with extremely thick parts in specific places, releasing to the wind a huge amount of free oxygen, but also with thinner parts that reach over almost all of the world's land, except for deserts and polar caps and the upper parts of high mountains (though the wind carries their pollen there too, however fruitlessly), and even grow abundantly in the oceans that cover most of the world.

Ocean plants as part of the Rainforest? Why not. Admitting them would stretch the word, but so did the word "rainforest" when it was coined just a little less than a century ago. "Forest" originally meant not just the trees that were home to deer and wild boars but the whole partially treed Outside that might include meadows with grazing sheep and even villages. All plants may fairly be thought included in a great encompassing forest of this kind, and they all need water as well as the wind that carries it. The ocean plants belong to our global Rainforest, especially since they give us even more free oxygen than the tree-dominated rainforests.

In the oceans, the tiny plants drift with the currents, moving and spreading across the world partly because of the way the wind steers the water; but nearly all the land-plants are permanently fixed where they first grew—and those that move, like the tumbleweed, depend entirely on the wind to do so. The wind brings to rooted or fixed plants the life that they cannot go anywhere to find. The wind carries the results of their living to the animals, who would otherwise die.

The great Rainforest is a truth that covers the whole world with plantlife and embraces all the animals within it, giving them the gift of life as well: because of the wind.

Animals, Plants, and Wind

"Animals" is a misleading name. It means something with a soul, an *animus;* something that can move, animated. But "soul," in its deepest meaning, is the principle of life in everything that lives.

Plants have life, and they have motion too: they grow, some of them shed and replace leaves, many of them push out blossoms and fruits, most of them either gestate seeds and release them or multiply through other tiny motions, such as the sprinkling or explosive tossing-out of spores. They move slowly, but they move; they live differently, but they are alive, and their life is far more like ours than we customarily think, even if they breathe backward.

Our ancestors knew that plants have souls, even if many of us have forgotten that truth. Many of the varied peoples of this present world still remember, more wisely than the rest of us, that plants are as genuinely alive and animated as we are, even if rather differently.

When we speak of rainforests, we usually mean not only the plants that compose them but also the animals that they shelter and sustain. If "rainforest" includes the "animals" that live among the living plants, and because of them, then "Rainforest" must include all of the world's intertwined life. That is what *Rainforest* really means: the complete complex of all living things. When we speak of the Rainforest, we should mean not only all the forms of plantlife that cover the earth but also the animals that live in their midst all over the globe, and are sustained by them. These two kinds of creatures as not so different that they should be named only separately. It is sometimes virtually impossible to tell them apart: the microscopic animals that are classed by the formidable name Phytomastigophora have chlorophyll and can photosysthesize as plants do. However one may choose to distinguish them, plants and animals are at the very least so dependent on one another that a single embracing name is more appropriate than the separate ones we customarily use. Taken all together (as they should be often, in order to be thought about more adequately and clearly), the plants and animals of the world make up the Rainforest, and *Rainforest* thus embraces all that lives, in delicate reciprocity.

Thinking the Wind

If the question is how animals are sustained, an important part of the answer is by plants. If the question is how plants are sustained, part of the answer is by animals. If the question is how life in general, the entire Rainforest, is sustained, *the answer is blowing in the wind.*

In some ancient languages—and some modern ones as well, though many of the modern ones have suffered distinctions that blot out the togetherbelongingness of things that are named—a single word served to name what ours calls spirit, breath, and wind. "Expire" can still mean either breathe out or die. "Inspire" has lost its hold on breathing-in, but can still be used that way at least in medical circles. We can still get the wind knocked out of us, or avoid long-winded speakers. Is it the wind or the spirit that "blows wherever it pleases?" Translators have to choose, but the original writer obviously liked the ambiguity in the language he or she used. A deftly chosen phrase in a speech in the 1960s caught on swiftly, and soon the "wind of change" blowing through Africa became almost as well established as the "iron curtain" that was rhetorically drawn across Europe some dozen years earlier. "Wind" blows through our language every which way: we get wind of things that are about to happen, run like the wind when speedy, get winded when we keep it up too long, place coming events in the wind, and lose whole cultures that are gone with it. We like windfalls, we dislike windbags. We play wind instruments by blowing through our windpipes, open and close windows (even windows of opportunity), reap whirlwinds, and (often for the better) end long paragraphs when we run out of wind.

The literal wind is even more pervasive than the metaphor, and far more important. *The wind goes everywhere, carrying the means of life and binding all life together. It reaches even the thinnest parts of the great Rainforest, the small plants that can survive above a mountain's timberline, the date-palms and tufts of grass around a small oasis, the lichens that cling to rocks amid glaciers, the patches of seaweed that stretch roots deep to the ocean floor and rise to where the wind nourishes the water. It reaches the surfacing seals in bone-chilling polar waters and the whales that surface in the seemingly bleak ocean where no land is within possible sight. It reaches, though more slowly, to moving fish and stationary shell-fish in the ocean depths, and through the surfaces of pools to minuscule "animals," some of which live by the wind's gifts through bodily parts that work more like the plants than like the rest of the animals. Distinctions become blurred, and nearly vanish. One truth remains presiding and unambiguous: where there is life, there is, or has recently been, wind.*

The Winds of the Windforest

*W*ithin the great prevailing winds that move, like some ocean currents, in one direction only, there are smaller breakaway winds that diverge, turn back, speed up, slow down, taking the refreshed air to all plants and animals. Within the smaller breakaway winds are still-smaller eddies, some of which break off into even smaller ones, until every leaf and lung is visited.

When all the winds are taken into account—*all* the winds, from the Prevailing Westerlies and the Jet Stream and the Monsoon to the delicate meadow breeze and the highdrift that moves rainbearing clouds so slowly that we can scarcely perceive its lifegiving presence, and all the way down to the tiny swirl that occurs when I move my finger slightly, or the almost unmeasurable airpush of a falling leaf that drifts pollen to its fruitfulness—they make up the vast, complex, multileveled, uninventoriable Windforest.

The Windforest has many prominent species, some of which are as world-famous as sequoias, oaks, baobabs, maples, and cedars, though not nearly as well-*known*. Nearly everyone has heard of the monsoon, though many of us have never felt one and might be hard put to say just when and where it happens. The westerlies are frequently mentioned, but even they are not popularly understood even by those who live in them (part of the confusion being that a westerly wind blows *from* the west, while a westerly ocean current flows *toward* the west). Trade winds are familiar enough to meteorologists to be called by the nickname "trades," but if you refer to "trades" in a general conversation, most of the participants will think that you are referring to particular occupations even if you meant something grander and more important to the world.

Many of the big winds are famous only locally, though the locale may be as extensive as the reach of the winds themselves. A simoom blows hot and dusty from any large desert, but the sirocco that visits southern France from the Sahara is a simoom that specializes enough to be predictable and will dominate weatherchat when in season, just as the mistral will do when it it blows cold to the same area from the opposite direction. The chinook and the Alberta Clipper are well known in the Upper Midwest; southern Californians all know the hot Santa Ana; the hamseen, which drives westward from the Arabian desert, makes a substantial impression on those it hits (as does the bora in the northern Adriatic), and the warm dry foehn (a close cousin of the chinook), which blows unpredictably in any season, makes enough difference to be recognized in Swiss law courts as an extenuating circumstance for irregular behavior.

Celebrating the Winds

*A*ll these major winds have their distinguishing per-
sonalities and particular behaviors, and deserve to
be recognized individually if only because of their practical effects—but we do not give them the notice they
merit: none of the winds mentioned in the previous

sentence appears in *The Oxford Dictionary of Current English*, even though it has over 140,000 entries and is generally hospitable to words of foreign origin. What chance of recognition can then be expected for the "Wisper wind" that the *Encyclopaedia Britannica* spots flowing down a Swiss valley to the Rhine, or the levanter that (according to *Britannica*) speeds above the straits of Gibraltar fast and strong enough to have interfered with low-flying air traffic in the opposite direction? "Jet stream" is English enough and important enough to qualify for the dictionary, but it isn't there, leaving readers to suppose that it has something to do with more successful airplanes. (It doesn't: it is a narrowed part of the prevailing westerlies and travels, with startling speed, well above the commercial jet planes whose pilots would not like to tangle with it and have avoided it since it was first discovered in 1944.)

Why should we be so unfamiliar with other special winds that bear names with the music of gregale, maestro, leveche, tramontana, pampero, etesian, khamsin, karaburan, abroholos, zonda, leste, kogarashi, tuaura, papagayos, shawondasee, tapayagua, and Euroclydon, or the abruptness of rok, klod, imbat, jauk, kwat, sz, and xlokk, or the more boistrous brickfielder, cockeye, schneefresser, black roller, frisk, williwaw, and burster? When we all recognize cyclone, tornado, and hurricane in the daily papers, why is it that so few know the differences? How is it that someone who has never left the county she was born in can name rivers all over the world, while a globetrotting diplomat or businessman is likely to run out of winds within the space of a single breath?

People old enough would be embarrassed if they failed to keep up with name-changes of countries when Siam and Dutch Guiana became Thailand and Surinam, one of the two Congos became Zaire, and Bechuanaland, Tanganyika, Southern Rhodesia, and various others changed their names though not their borders. We were not thrown off when The Gold Coast was renamed and its next-door neighbor The Ivory Coast was not, and Burma's decision to become Myanmar is rapidly getting installed in our habits. We weathered the transitions when most of India's Bengal became first East Pakistan and then Bangladesh; even the bewilderingly complex transformation of Indochina to Laos, Cambodia, and Vietnam (the latter subsequently divided into North and South, like Korea, then rejoined again) was taken in stride.

Many of the world's countries have changed their borders as well as their names, and both the old and the new borders are often rather arbitrary historical accidents rather than following major rivers, mountain ranges, and language groups; but we accept them as they have been drawn or redrawn. We expect ourselves to know even the capital cities, and will adjust to the change in Nigeria's as we did in Brazil's, and educated peoples of other lands will eventually recognize that Canada's is neither Montreal nor Toronto.

The United Nations of Winds

The names of nations are historically accidental and arbitrary by comparison with the dominant members of the Windforest, which have appropriately personal names that are rarely used or even known, despite their having been steadily there longer than humanity has. The more local winds also antedate the human population, but they usually remain anonymous outside the places where they blow. And that is not even taking account of an incalculable number of winds that have probably never been named at all, unlike the plants and animals of the Rainforests, which are normally named by the natives therein and are eagerly renamed as rapidly as they come to scientific notice. (The painkilling Ecuadorean frog is *Epibpedobates tricolour,* but no such resounding name is given to its rainforest nor to the winds that sustain it.) When winds whose lifespans rival or surpass those of some nations go without identifying names, there is little chance for the naming of the more whimsical and unpredictable winds that live as briefly as mayflies. Hurricanes get named, and make the news accordingly during the few weeks or days before they vanish; but not tornadoes, despite the strong impression they can make in their ephemeral careers. General type-names (breeze, windstorm, blizzard, squall, gust, gale) are far too crude to pay respect to the differentiations among them—as if in dealing with colors, we could say only yellow, red, and blue-green, and qualify them only with light and dark. There are probably more species in the Windforest than there are in Rainforest monkeys, and obviously more than there are nations. So why are we so negligent about discriminating the membership of the Windforest?

Much of the answer is obvious. No one sends ambassadors, trade commissioners, sales representatives, or tourists to the Windforest or any of its distinguishable parts. The political boundaries imposed by us on the Rainforest, however arbitrary and temporary they may be, have practical implications. Botanists and zoologists have been eagerly classifying and naming plant and animal species ever since Linnaeus gave us a rationalized systematic way of doing so more than two centuries ago, and their work is not only of practical importance but is theoretically significant as well.

Everybody talks about the weather, but hardly anyone does anything about studying the winds that govern it. Fortunately the few that do have made a great difference in our ability to understand and track hurricanes, send out tornado warnings, predict rain for endangered crops (and sometimes even make it happen), and explain El Niño (La Niña is much neglected by comparison); but the study is still at a rudimentary stage. We know more about chromosomes and DNA, and dinosaurs and pre-life rocks, than we do about the Windforest. Our ignorance about the Windforest contributes to the perpetuation of that ignorance far more than it stumulates its remedy. That is not only unfair: it is unreal. We are governed by powers that we do not elect, and cannot persuade or overthrow.

Turmoil and Taming

*T*here is another reason for the neglect of the Wind-forest, though it is hardly a justification: it eludes understanding. It does so in almost every possible way. It reaches to the utter limits of the world, well beyond where we could examine it until very recently, and it gets invisibly into the tiniest and most secret nooks— and wherever it goes, it is constantly changing.

It is notorious that local weather can be predicted for at most a few days in advance, and there are lots of little jokes about the hapless weatherman. That is because the Windforest is far more unstable than the Rainforest, hence far more unpredictable. A Climate is somewhat like personal character or the policies of a stable government, containing many variables but tending to regulate them into overall dominating patterns. Climate used to be considered the constant at the other end of the spectrum from inconstant weather, but is now known to be hardly more consistent than governments, and quite capable of being out of character. Weather is more like a volatile personality, or a family where spontaneously erupting squalls and gusts can destabilize an apparent equilibrium in minutes, and may require a radical reorganization to meet the new forces. *After two warm and sunny days in a given neighborhood, the breaking-off of a huge iceberg a thousand miles away can start a movement of air that may gather more strength as it travels and poof! The balmy afternoons are gone with the wind. Especially with the wind. Who could have known?*

The study of chaos is a relatively recent fashion. Where most studies concentrate on isolating features that are regular and constant, chaos-studies look to the randomnesses that make the picture far less tidy. Poke and probe far enough into any aspect of the Rainforest, and you will find chaotic happenings among and beneath the regular surfaces, variations that defy every attempt at systematic explanation. The standard model for a system that is blatantly chaotic is weather, but it should be *Windforest.*

That of course would give the Windforest a bad reputation among people who like to settle their understandings conclusively. Mathematics, chemistry, and physics are in much higher esteem as studies than psychology, sociology, and politics. Mechanisms and abstractions behave in a rather orderly fashion. Where there is life, there is intellectually bothersome irregularity, and human life is by far the most irregular of all forms. The Windforest has an interesting place midway between: theoretically, its forces are mechanical and could be reduced to a comprehensive abstracted system, but its actual behavior is so free and multifarious and interpenetrating that it baffles the minds that attempt to master it, even more than governments that fall and companies that fail despite their attempts to use all the tools of sociology, psychology, and politics to win elections or sell products. It is easier to study the Han dynasty, now that what it consisted of has been said and done and stopped happening, than to get a sound grasp on the real condition of China yesterday morning, let alone predicting tomorrow evening. If we could name and know *exactly* how the entire Windforest is dynamically structured at the moment of the first cock-crow in Nebraska on the next Labor Day, most of it would be useless by the end of the week and indeed, the overall picture would be significantly out of date by the fourth cock-crow.

Irregular; unpredictable; disorderly; unstable; chaotic. The first four are obviously evaluations as well as descriptions, since they are made by negating the convenient and desirable qualities of being stable, orderly, predictable, and regular. "Chaotic" is not built the same way but is virtually always used as the strongest and most hopeless extreme of ruinous breakdown. We have a huge and unfortunate bias against conditions to which these words may be applied.

There are some familar words that question or suspend the bias: unconstrained, boundless, indomitable, unconventional, irrepressible, fortuitous, lucky, inventive, liberated, spontaneous, *free*. But for all our celebrations of freedom, we tend to place a much higher value on regularity and the regulation by which it can be imposed, and the words at the beginning of the previous paragraph get much more serious use than the ones in the previous sentence. We acknowledge that there are a few problems that haven't been solved yet, but we like to think that they are all soluble, and that the solutions are fairly close, only a few scientific experiments away. We indulge our romanticism by celebrating what remains of the Wild, including the rainforests, but that is largely because we can put it on display like a geographically dispersed zoo where wild patches are safely contained within the surrounding and dominant Tamed. The identifiable Wild gets visited, but few decide to stay there. We have a strong and understandable preference for the Tamed as our usual habitat.

We prefer the Tamed so strongly, in fact, that we strive to do more taming everywhere outside the protected wild preserves; and although we enjoy visits to the curtailed surprises of sanitized wildspots (often making them more convenient by sacrificing part of their wildness to the invasive building of safely regulated restaurants and tidy motels), we do not like to think of *our* part of the Rainforest as being as wild as it really is. Those who bother to think about the world at large prefer to see it as an extraordinarily sophisticated and complex mechanism that our descendants may at last understand *completely* if they follow the trail we have blazed through the breaking of the DNA code, the inspection of the Big Bang, the discovery of black holes and the structures of viruses and atoms, and the great manifestations of these accomplishments in the first unmythical man-in-the-moon, a cloned sheep, and an almost unbelievably destructive bomb. The image of a great human mind is no longer the Wise Old Woman or the Philosopher: the touchstone has become the "rocket scientist."

Much of this is technically unreal as well as regrettably misplaced. Like the man in the old story, who searches for his lost housekey under the streetlamp because the light is better there than in the park where he knows he dropped it, we have invested a disproportionate amount of our mental and material resources, and our admiring attention, in the pursuit of what is easier to label and control than the facts of *life*. Meanwhile, a steady look into the Rainforest discloses a bewildering complexity that discourages the hope of exhaustive understanding. And even a glance into the Windforest shows it to be ultimately inscrutable. That may inspire a measure of awed respect, but it also rouses our decided preference for scrutability. Off to the lamppost: the key is not there, but there is more to be seen, quite enough to reward the available time by pinning a few things down even if not quite enough time to bring home the realization that the relatively stable Rainforest too is finally inscrutable, and the Windforest only minutes away from baffling our last attempt to grasp how it ensouls the world.

A Reconsideration of Prejudice

Prejudices are not all bad. Many of us find it useful to be biased against the assumption that all the burners on the stove are cool, and against a building that bravely rents apartments on the thirteenth floor but straddles the San Andreas fault, and against proposals made by apparently sincere and likeable and sympathetic people who offer a way of becoming fabulously rich by investing a relatively small number of used and unmarked banknotes.

But we are all agreed in promoting a prejudice against prejudices. Some are helpful, but most of them are decidedly limiting. They bring the comfort of order, regularity, stability, and self-fulfilling predictability, but not on the whole for the better. Liberation from them is not cheap release; one pays a real price in the loss of confidence and contentment that always attends the evaporation of prejudices, because they protected values, however misleadingly. Once we remove familiar and unthreatening prejudicial facades, we must confront new imponderables that were hidden behind them. Still, if one is willing to pay that considerable price in order to be more adequately attuned to reality—and not everyone would consider it inexorbitant, let alone a bargain—there are wonderful and reassuring realizations that compensate for the surrender of tidiness.

We should abandon the prejudice against disorder. That does not entail becoming objectionably disorderly; it merely raises one's level of tolerance and opens the way to revaluations of disorderly realities that we are used to disapproving of, trivializing, or even refusing to acknowledge, though they are sometimes just what we need to adjust to. Or, to put it more comprehensively, it moves us into a Reality that is immeasurably more ineffable and eccentric than we are used to supposing it, and gives us a chance to see it as richer than the way we had stylized it, much more abundant in significant opportunities for all of us, *transcending* order rather than merely failing to conform, and constantly inviting us to be more real than we are.

It is a pity that we have so few language-resources for redescribing more adequately the resources that abide, however unpredictably, within our Rainforest. "Chaos" could mean immeasurable possibility, but won't: the best we can do to disinfect the prejudices that "chaos" carries is to understand it as the wild Big Bang from which a cosmos was composed to tame it. That at least admits chaos as an initial resource, but also makes it seem to be mainly the biggest thought-problem in the history of the universe, now on the way to being solved. We need a name for the ongoing abundance of spontaneous and unpredictable possibilities that will precisely stand *against* the word "chaos" as a way of renaming what is multifariously and extravagantly there and releasing us to its appreciative acknowledgement.

There is a name, and a coordinate reality, that will help. It is "Windforest." The contemplation of the Windforest can give us a mirror-reflection of the true shape of the Rainforest that embraces and fosters all life. But the Windforest is not merely a mirror: we will eventually realize that it is a soul.

Spiritus Mundi

*I*t is the Windforest that makes the Rainforest possible. It is the Windforest that gives and sustains the Rainforest's life.

We rarely try to see the Windforest, and in fact we cannot do so. When we try to see what it mirrors, it is the *perfect mirror—invisible in itself but known through what it reflects. It seems to be visible in the driving blizzard and in the ominous funnel of a tornado, but even there we see only what it carries in its intense swirl, not a part of the Windforest itself: a "white tornado" is one that has not yet picked up passengers, and is as invisible as an airpocket.*

The Windforest reveals itself only by its effects. But its effects are everywhere. We can see the churning and crashing of ocean waves and know the invisible vigor of the Windforest that masters them. We can see the illusory blue sky and the illusory twinkle of the stars, and know that we are looking into and through the unseeable Windforest, and that both the blue and the twinkling belong to it. We can see the Rainforest thrive, and know that this is because of the secret hidden work of the Windforest. Sometimes it reveals itself to our ears and our skin, though usually it is too delicate to be felt or heard. It has no taste or smell, even if it can waft flavors and odors to us over great distances.

The Windforest penetrates almost everything in the Rainforest; and what it does not reach is reached by what the Windforest has provided. The self-interpenetration of the Rainforest is mainly a function of the Windforest that makes it possible as it breaks down boundaries and distinctions. Forensic science has become skillful in identifying the proper homeplace of even lifeless soil, allowing prosecutors to say that these shoes once walked in northern New Jersey and that car has been a little south of Mexico City. But a still more exacting examination of the soil of those places would show that, far from enjoying (or enduring) isolation, they bear traces of dust from Hawaii, the Sahara, and far-distant Indonesia's volcano Krakatoa. The microscope will also show bits of pollen that were originally released to the wind in central Africa, the upper Amazon basin, and southeastern Australia. The Windforest can make everywhere present anywhere. Even more spectacularly, it can arrange that traces of your body can appear in mine, and vice versa, and that our lives are intermingled with lives lived all over the world. *The Windforest is the giver and sustainer of the Rainforest's abundant life as well as the means by which the byproducts of living are universally shared. It is the conquerer of inanimate space and time, and it is the soul of the living world.*

Taking in the Breath of the Windforest

The Windforest shows all the signs of life even though is not itself alive. It moves constantly, and with dazzling versatility. It replicates senescence and birth, and its members beget progeny that both resemble them and differ from them. Its discernible parts die, and are reborn. It acts both more powerfully and more delicately than any living thing, but is not itself alive. Still, all life is alive because of it. So while it is true to say that the Windforest has no life, it is perhaps more true to say that it has the life of everything that lives. The truth of the Windforest is perhaps too deep to name adequately. Its inadequate name is perhaps sufficient: Windforest.

Whisper it gently: Windforest. However gentle your whisper, it becomes a part of the Windforest it names. However small its contribution to the Windforest, your whisper changes it; and no one can know how much difference that change, however absurdly small, may make in the rest of the Rainforest's life.

A leaf falls in a rainforest, stirring the air even less than your whisper; but this tiny moment of the Windforest may be enough to waft pollen where it would not otherwise go, and fertilize a blossom that will produce a unique mutation of a tree whose descendants will be immune to a disease that will destroy all its other relatives seven centuries later, giving the mutant trees room to reconstitute the entire rainforest. You never know. Not knowing doesn't always matter.

In a Zen Temple

We are in the Temple's meditation hall. We who
are gathered there are all as silent and unmoving
as can be. The door and windows are closed, but the
room is not sealed. It is extremely difficult to seal a
room so well that the resourceful Windforest cannot

enter. No one has tried to seal this room, only to close it against disturbing noise. If we try, we can hear the sounds of traffic outside, delicate footsteps above made by people trying to walk as gently as they can, an occasional birdcall or the scrambling of a squirrel. I try not to listen, concentrating my attention elsewhere. I cannot hear any part of the Windforest, but I know that if sounds can reach me from outside the room, the Windforest can too. Sound travels by way of the Windforest, and even changes it slightly, though usually too slightly to detect except by results that may not be evident until years after the sound's echo has died away and no memory of it remains except in the Windforest itself.

I cannot even hear the quiet breathing of the others, even if I try. Most of the time, I cannot hear even my own breath. But I know that we are all breathing, and that the Windforest is alive within the room and that it will take some of the breaths out through the cracks around the door into the world outside the room, just as our silent breathing will draw new parts of the Windforest into the room in the same way. In our silence, we are all still joined to the rest of the world through the Windforest.

Before we all fell silent, we were asked to focus our minds on our breathing. *Count it,* the leader said. *Count your breaths to five, or to thirty-six. That is all you have to do. If your mind wanders, just bring it back and resume counting breath.*

We try naming our breath with numbers. I try doing nothing else with my body and mind except breathing and naming my breath with numbers. I try letting go of the numbers, and focusing only on the truth of breathing. My mind wanders to the truth that I am not only a breathing, I am not only breath. I try to pull back to the breathing itself, the breath alone, but my body tells me that there is more going on that I perhaps ought not to try to ignore.

I can feel the rhythmic pulsing of my blood, though I cannot hear it. I know that my breath is adding moisture to the Windforest's presence within the room, and my pores are silently and motionlessly adding more, along with bodily scents, heat that will slightly affect the air-currents, a touch of coffee-flavor from just before I left home, microscopic bits of nutrients that my body has been breaking down since yesterday for its own benefit and has been spreading generously about within me, so liberally that some of it will be escaping through lungs and pores and breath into this room's corner of the Windforest. There will be germs too, possibly some that might be potentially harmful to others in the room, certainly some that assist in breaking down food for bodily use and might turn out to be helpful to others. Maybe even infinitesimal material that will help others to build resistance against harmful germs. I pull my mind back to naming my breath with numbers.

But my mind drifts again, like the Windforest itself, and I notice in my mind what I could not notice in any other way, that my breath is taking in what the others are giving out: their carbon dioxide, some free oxygen that has been within their bodies but not caught by their lungs, bits of their breakfasts, a few expired touches of cologne, shampoo, lotions, medications, laundry detergent, toothpaste, cosmetics, foodstains, tobacco, mouthwash, cola—all too feeble to detect, but certainly there. Someone coughs or sneezes: that changes everything, however slightly. New bits of the recent past are set free and everything stirred up more. New germs, some wholesome, some unwelcome, some neutral, collectively few enough that they will probably make no difference to me except in my realization that the Windforest makes us participate in one another despite our closed eyes and silence and untouching separation and differently focused minds. I bring mine back again to my breath, but now everyone is there. *I am breathing them, because there is no other way to breathe within the Windforest. Might it be better to notice this than to concentrate on getting an aloneness that is less than true?*

In the Temple, Failing

I try again to name my breathing with numbers, but the numbers have become obtrusive. They have become mindclutter. I try to think of nothing at all, reaching for perfect emptiness; but thought is swirling just out of reach, like the Windforest, and it is no good to pretend that it isn't there. It doesn't even work to treat it as if it doesn't intrude: even if it only whispers, too gently for me to hear with my mind's withheld ear, I know by its expression and its gesture at me what it is whispering about. It is whispering about the Windforest. Just as it has made its way into my body, with no possible way of keeping it out, the Windforest has made its way into my mind. What can I do about this? How can I seal my mind's door against it so that I can meditate? How can I rise above it to the purity of complete emptiness?

Frustrated, I let go of my striving to let go. Then of course the Windforest returns to fill the pretended void in my mind, and becomes my meditation. I know that it had never left. At best, it just maintained its usual quiet way of being there without making a fuss big enough to be noticed. But it seems to like being noticed; or at least I like noticing it, though I appreciate that I don't *have* to do so: it doesn't howl or bang my shutters when I want to concentrate on something else.

Now that I give it hospitality, the meditative exploring of the Windforest begins to fill my mind just as the Windforest itself fills the Rainforest. I begin to welcome it as my getting in touch with its truth. It grows to fill my thought as it fills the world. It is mainly friendly and comforting, as I gradually get over worrying about the fact that there is no way of escaping it. Oh yes, it warns me of its dangers and quirks, all the way from hurricanes to drifting diseases, but I notice indelibly that the Windforest is not only utterly true but utterly indispensable as well, the giver and sustainer of all life even if occasionally erupting with destructive power and capable of insinuating what is harmful along with what is needful.

As I wander the Windforest in my mind, trying to follow the paths by which it wanders into my body, I notice truths that I had not adequately noticed before: for better or for worse, it is always faithfully there; it is always faithfully *here*; it is always bringing there to here and back again, intermingling the counted or uncounted breaths, intermingling the breaths of the unsealed room with what is outside it, eventually intermingling all living things and all life.

The Temple, Winddrift

A whiff of incense, perhaps confected a year ago, far
away, by an old woman whose grandmother taught
her how. Imperceivable specks of dust blown loose long
ago halfway around the planet. The Windforest masters
time as well as space: what happened in the Han dynasty

is not entirely over after all—nothing is ever completely finished, nothing vanishes altogether, however bewildering it may be to ponder this.

I begin to get caught up in the Windforest. No, I *am* caught up in the Windforest, and begin to realize it. As I realize and wander and realize more, the horizons of my mind drop and spread so that I begin to sense directly a much larger world than I saw from the foot of the hill. *It is all bound together as a self-uniting world through the Windforest. There is no void, no empty place, within the sealed world of the world itself. Everything interpenetrates everything else. Everything alive shares itself with everything else alive. Because of the Windforest, everything affects everything else. There is nothing that happens that is too small to make a difference.*

That is a rather unsettling realization. Good differences may spread and multiply, mutate and burgeon, but so can bad ones. Anything I do will immediately escape my control; no amount of vigilance on my part can keep me from doing damage, and as the damage spreads it is entirely beyond my capacity to control or even identify the harm for which I am ultimately responsible. I can scarcely distinguish the likely damage from the likely good at the moment I act, and no filter can keep the effects as wholesome as I intend them to be, not even in my most careful doings. I cannot escape by not doing: no living thing can not-do, and inaction can be as irresponsibly harmful as malicious doing.

"If you become pure and innocent," the leader said as the meditation started, *"your land and society will become pure and innocent as well and to the same degree."* So what follows if purity and innocence are simply out of the question, beyond any thinkable possibility, totally overruled by the truth of the Windforest? *"If you become happy and peaceful, your land and society will become happy and peaceful . . . ."* But how can what the Windforest tells me leave me at peace, when even as I count my breaths harmlessly I am emitting harm, and old damage is still reverberating out there troubling the peace of others? And if my land is all land, my society all society, how can the world's unhappiness and pain not trouble my waters unless I extinguish compassion and pretend falsely that all the world's wind is not drawn in with my breath?

I breathe in deeply, not counting. I breathe in traces of hurt and anxiety and grief and fear and hatred and despair and loneliness from all over the world. I do not like the way it smells to my mind, but no incense is strong enough to blot it out. I feel more troubled and disturbed rather than more happy and peaceful.

Obviously, my meditation has gone wrong. Less obviously, it has perhaps gone right. Am I entitled to decide? Maybe not; but as I return to the leader's words, I cannot see their truth because I cannot feel the promised stillness. They now seem a hedge that brakes the wind, bringing calm, but the wind still seeps through them, eddies around them, and in the relative calm the air is still gently alive with what the wind has carried: truths that call the comforting words into question and blow them askew. The room is not sealed. There is no place that is entirely safe. We have been asked to abandon illusions. The Windforest tells me that one of the illusions that I must abandon is the illusion of safety, untainted happiness and peace, hermetic seal against unsettling truths, even the meditative isolation of this room from all other rooms and spaces, and each of us meditative breathers from the others whom we deliberately do not see but breathe in all the same. I hear another sneeze: it will make far more difference than the glances that we withhold from one another.

What can I do about the truths that the Windforest blows to me, and into me? Or *from* me, for that matter? Painfully little. But even that realization is not unqualifiedly painful. It would be selfish and unreal, and terribly smallminded, to wish to control the differences I have made. I cannot grow wise enough to do it well even if it were possible, since I can have only a shabby understanding of how these differences will reverberate beyond my reach, beyond my life, or what values they will gain or lose in the process. It is something of a relief to realize that it is flatly, even ludicrously, impossible to control them: I am not equipped to take that kind of responsibility. Of course, it would be even more selfish, unreal, and smallminded *not* to take care that the happenings I originate will make good differences and avoid harmful ones, but I cannot even see to that: some harm will inevitably arise somewhere as a result of every action, however carefully screened and evaluated. Having little wisdom of my own, I turn to the wisdom of the Windforest, and it tells me that there is not very much I can do about all that: I should do what I can, but avoid the illusion that I can become harmless, or even take satisfying credit for doing good.

And so too with others: if this one were easy to get along with rather than being as difficult as he is, I would know less about my limitations and see less adequately how I need to change; if that one had not hurt me deeply, I would not have found out how unfairly I leaned on her to affirm me; if those others had not been such caricatured and dangerous specimens of bigotry, I would not have realized how much I too am tainted with the same distortions. If we did not blunder conspicuously, we would grow unrealistically smug about the adequacy of who we are. If we are not heard, we can learn to listen as well as how to say louder and more clearly. If others suffer pain and ignorance and abuse, we gain perspective about our own discomforts and entitlements and obligations. Even an ill wind can blow some good.

Everyone belongs to everyone, everything belongs to everything. The Windforest is at work, more vastly and more intimately than I can follow, carrying happenings over space and time as they change their colors and values uncontrollably for better and for worse. The Windforest in my mind is at work, making a difference: it is changing my way of seeing and thinking, it is changing my ability to receive and accept, it is changing my willingness to give and belong, it is changing my sense of my significance, my deserving, my indebtedness, my responsibility, my world. The change is still tiny, like the falling leaf, but the Windforest has begun blowing me home.

What the Windforest tells me is not all good news. Home is neither the place where I am safe nor the place where I am meant to be comfortable. It is where I really live, and both comfort and safety are dangerous illusions. I want to see and accept it more adequately, not to become happy and peaceful but to become more real, and therefore more authentically restless.

In the Temple, in the Wind

*A*mid this morning's breakfasts, yesterday's beer and onions and hairspray, last week's laundries, and the incense that may trace back to a woman who is still abjectly poor, I long for relief and forgetting.

There is no such thing, and my longing is the cry of a child unready for the truth. I try remembering.

The woman who boarded the elevator on—the eighth floor? whatever—as I descended had a small laundry basket that she held up as she pressed two, the floor with the laundry room, and then settled silently into a corner until she left at two without a word or a glance back. But as she had entered the elevator, she had looked right at me briefly and smiled Good Morning. I had only returned a small token nod, being a bit preoccupied. But somehow, as the elevator descended, her smile had begun to get through and light me up a little. I passed a man waiting for an elevator on the ground floor, and then two more people on the way to the subway, and instead of the usual urban pretending that they weren't there, I greeted them with my eyes. I couldn't see a reaction, but probably the woman on the elevator couldn't see mine, which was withheld too long. I paused at the corner store for some mints (now shared in the room though perhaps unnoticed) and not only said "thank you" to the clerk but actually *thanked* her. The seed from the elevator, though undeserved, was coming into bloom. I carried it past the ticket booth and dropped an unseen smile on the man within, who was stacking coins and couldn't notice. No matter. I took it into the subway car and shared it with the three or four people who looked up. I was feeling strangely happy, and my earlier preoccupation lifted as I looked around the subway car, admiring others' preoccupied faces and wishing that I had a way of effectively wishing them well, and then abandoned wishing to take on a determination to give them what I had already gratuitously received. No one looked up; I kept my usual mannerly distance with disappointment. By the time we arrived at the station, the blossom had started to fade, and by the time I entered the meditation hall I was my old unlit self again. But ". . . for twenty minutes, more or less, I felt that I was blessed, and could bless." I knew that it was true. I did not succeed in enacting it.

Remembering, I now start lighting up again, grateful for contagious spontaneity, knowing that I will remember this again, hopeful that the planted seed will reawaken whenever I do, wondering at the way in which a moment of spontaneous greeting from a stranger can start something that may keep echoing, and snowballing, as long as life itself endures. *In the embrace of the Windforest, a single falling leaf might change the Rainforest forever.*

I myself am here by a convergence of fortuitous accidents. *What* I am that is worth passing onward is almost all a version of what I have received abundantly from those who went before me, bequeathed to me by my mother, my grandfather, ancestors whose names are nowhere remembered anymore, people of distant centuries and places that no longer exist—the builders of language and the tamers of fire, those who made melodies and recipes and new ways of expressing friendship, those who discouraged slavery and conquered diseases and opposed gratuitous hurtfulness and in their own ways remedied the neglect of children's feelings.

I turn with the wind in another direction, and look at the darker side. All of us were polluted by the same process that empowered us, and the vastness of what needs to be undone, including the damage I am responsible for and cannot eradicate, would be too overwhelming to face without the realization that the Windforestly disorder can overcome the doom of ordered causality. Beyond the debris left by the effects of negligence and selfishness and malice and greed lies a vast and messy world of possibility that we have only begun to build and leaven, an irregularlly windflung reservoir of potential resources for cherishing and fostering the life that will be nourished and connected by the Windforest for as long as we allow it, a life to which each of us may bequeath, even in the smallest gesture, new eddies of happening that will be unnameably lost from view but whose effects will unstoppably continue as long as . . . .

Another Changing

*I*n the very, very unsealed meditation hall, the bell implodes the silence. We rise, bow reverently toward a statue representing a man who was no rocket scientist but has pulled us here together from well over two thousand years ago, and file out silently, seemingly disconnected from one another and averting our eyes until we have left the hall. I reenter another part of the Windforest; another part of the Windforest reenters me more immediately. It is gusty, but that is a trivial and superficial truth, though I button up my jacket. I carry the Windforest, and it carries me, out to the street, where I must turn my attention to catching a steetcar and deciding whether to go directly home or do a trivial errand that will require a stopoff and a glance at a map as well as at my watch.

I have not left the Windforest any more than it has left me. Much less, in fact, as I now realize. I cannot leave it. I would not wish to leave it even if it were possible without dying. I have left only my concentration on it, but it faithfully continues to concentrate on me, and on the woman who was at my left in the meditation hall, and on the man who rang the bell, and on every living being in the great sealed self-supporting utterly interconnected world. I can return my attention to it, more or less, on the streetcar, after I have checked out some trivial matters of time and space. But then, that may turn out not to be so trivial after all. I will probably never know. I don't need to know. I need only to live gratefully and consciously in my place in the Windforest, a place that fortunately cannot be privately occupied.

The Windforest will always be here, hospitable to further exploration. It has finally drifted into my mind, and will always be there too. I am only a beginner at consciously living in the Windforest, but I know that it is good to have begun and that I will keep beginning over and over as I wander in it over the coming years. The streetcar arrives. It too rings a bell. I start to board, taking a rich deep breath. I suddenly realize that I did not count as I did so: I only smiled, first to myself and then to the driver as I offered my ticket. She smiled back. Who knows what we started, or where the wind will blow it?

The Misleading Lightness of Elation

$\mathcal{I}$t would be unrealistically sentimental to leave it there, as if the truth is simply that one small candle can light a thousand more. True, but trivially true. One small candle once burned down Chicago. The exchange of smiles is not a specially pure and privileged happening that can only bring good to the world. The proverb that points out that a wind with bad effects almost certainly benefits *someone* deserves to be counterbalanced by another saying that even the balmiest breeze will not universally please. Had the driver and I just played our respective roles, I merely paying my fare efficiently and moving out of others' way and she making sure that I wasn't cadging a free ride or lingering cloggingly at the front, the event would be more neutralized and the needs of public transportation better served. The gratuitous smiles were disorderly, and anyone who has explored the Windforest must know that this is not unusual and not necessarily good. Still, her smile seemed real, and my heart rose again.

I did not want to question this privileged moment, but I felt the need to question the privilege. For all I know, the exchange of smiles may have inspired envy and resentment in a passenger who saw it, thinking "Why did *she* get a smile when I didn't? feminist disdain? white in-group solidarity? I don't look worthy of friendliness?" The driver may eventually have been plunged into a contagious bad mood, reproving herself for having been momentarily tricked into a meaningless pretense that something worthwhile was happening, me trying to treat the moment as a significant human encounter when the reality was that I was just another passenger and she was just doing her job when she would rather be home with a child whom she must neglect in order to make a living by being a uniformed servant to people who can afford a monthly pass: the smile she had answered, my smile, was possibly—prob-ably?—patronizing and demeaning, and she had let herself be gulled into playing my little game.

And *was* I playing a little game? I guess that the answer has to be at least "Probably, even if not en-tirely," and for a more adequate one I would have to turn to "Yes, even though some real values smuggled themselves in all the same." I was getting her to smile. I was showing off how nice I am. I was playing not my proper role as dutiful passenger but the affected role of someone who has just grown terribly wise and gener-ous—oh, and remarkably humble and unpretentious too—as a result of a classy visit to a meditation session on a Sunday morning when *I* don't have to go to work but can indulge myself by showing that I am above watching morning TV or sleeping in.

One of the lessons of the Windforest is that if there is pollution out there, it will find you; and another one is that part of the pollution was your own distinctive contribution. Purity is another of the illusions that fa-miliarity with the Windforest will tend to blow away. Mountain air is cleaner, by the standards our limited bodies dictate, than city smog; but it has its own share of unwholesome byproducts, and is contaminated fur-ther by my breathing in it. There is no escape. Perfectly unselfish motivation is about as common as *total* dark-ness (try to find a place free of infrared light) and spon-taneous vacuums; complete honesty is attainable only in conversations that take place either in germ-free kitchens or at a temperature of absolute zero; anyone who is too moral to consider accepting dirty money, money that has been associated with some form of wrongdoing, will never be able to cash a paycheck.

Instability and disorder eventually spread contamination at least as efficiently as systematic destructiveness does, and usually much more thoroughly. But contamination is not itself a terminal illness. We can survive a lot of it. And some of it works changes for the better. The worst wine comes from batches corrupted by strong windborne wild yeasts that outperform the chosen ones; but the very best wine derives from strong windborne wild yeasts too, carefully protected and nurtured through generations of vintages once the original random wind has made its distinctive mark on new possibilities. Without the steady regularity of the seasons that ride on the winds, we would not have the grapes in the first place; but without the random whimsies of the Windforest we would have neither poor wines nor great ones, and would be lucky to be able to settle for mildly contaminated and somewhat soured grape juice.

We are not held hostage to unpredictablility and chaotic instability, even if the entire Rainforest, echoing the Windforest, is inextricably shot through with such irregularity from its seeds and roots to its blossoms and fruits. As chaos theorists have realized, a highly unstable unsystem like the Windforest generates not only unanticipatable and random forces that bring further disturbance but also unanticipatable and random other forces that counterbalance them. The total complex eventually develops not a systematic and rationalizable order, but a sort of pulsating equilibrium with too many variables to track but also with discernible limits at every margin, beyond which the complex will not trespass.

What students of chaos call a "strange attractor" names the outer boundary of the disordering tendencies, the limit imposed on each of them by the others and turns them together into a system of happenings that is self-limiting rather than self-destructing. Within that outer boundary, special conditions establish sub-boundaries for subsystems. In the Windforest, for instance, a place designated by a specific longitude and latitude will usually have fairly stable topographical features, at least if we measure on the limited scale of hundreds of thousands of years; and when just these three variables (many others are also in play, of course) are taken into consideration, we can form a rather reliable notion of what the Windforest will and will not do in that neighborhood at a given time of year. The plants and animals of the Rainforest can take advantage of that imitation of stability, and in time are likely to adapt themselves to be so good at doing so that they may survive only with difficulty, or not at all, if transposed to another place.

Our particular species is not as good (or self-limiting) at specialized adaptation as, say, koalas and pandas, who dine at one restaurant only and perish if it closes. Being ourselves more randomized, we are more generally adaptable, and there are very few parts of the globe where the Windforest has not been directly enriched and contaminated by human breath, and not many parts where that phenomenon is not a regular fixture.

But adaptability is not our only advantage. At least as important is our ability to cultivate.

Cultivation

*L*ocation, location, and location are the three major considerations for ambitious wines as well as struggling businesses. But neither of them can thrive on location alone. Both businesses and vines must be cultivated, deliberately adjusted to the location's possibities rather than waiting through centuries for the consolidation of spontaneous adaptations. Cultivation is very close to being the ultimate inner boundary for the Windforest of the world and the Windforest of the mind.

On the largest scale of human substystem management, this cultivation takes the form of Politics—not in the limited sense of competition for election but in the more comprehensive view of Aristotle's *Politics*: the ordering of a community toward the highest and greatest good. His very politically conscious Athenian community invested a great deal of thought, by minds that continue to astound us with their enduring insights, in this dimension of cultivation. They produced searching political thinking that can serve as an efficent metaphor: there is no way to cultivate the strongest form of order in combination with a constitutional guarantee of the freedom of individual lives, and no way to cultivate freedom and self-determination without giving rise to the messiness of conflicting interests and a propensity to instability.

As a system, a society—especially if perceived not only in political terms, but also in social ways that include the level of smiles and snubs, harsh and soothing words, giving and withholding—is probably the most irregular and disorderly complex that the universe affords, since each of the elements that compose it has a much higher level of free self-determination and a much lower level of subjection to determining forces than any other. That makes its cultivation difficult, especially since the taming of it must be designed and implemented and enacted and modulated by the somewhat wild components themselves. There can be no ideal of social order that will not be in some ways disappointing. All values are secured at the expense of others. No implemented ideal of justice can succeed in being just, even according to its own terms. Collision, dissatisfaction, contamination, failure are always with us, like windblown weeds. We must cultivate imperfectly.

The same is true of individual lives. It is simply unrealistic to adopt an ideal of avoiding all harmdoing. Righteousness is not attainable within a human life any more than the Windforest can exist without doing damage. In the Windforest of the mind, significant error, inadequate attention, and blundering judgment can never be purged. But they can be identified and reduced, named and tamed.

The best we can do is to cultivate as wisely as we can. Voltaire's Candide ends his exploration through the world and its societies with advice that looks similar: after all is said and done and seen and heard, we must cultivate our own garden. But this comes as a counsel of rather cynical defeat, though slightly upbeat in its offer of at least *something* to be done to stave off personal poverty, vice, and boredom. The Windforest means, and sees to it, that there is no private garden, that riches abound, and that boredom is not a legitimate complaint but a confession of unappreciativeness.

My garden, like yours, receives from and gives to all the world, whether we take account of this or not. We must cultivate our most immediate portions of the great Rainforest garden as our special shares of a distributed common task, but we would do it better if we keep up the realization that it is a part of that common task, taking place within a part of that great encompassing garden that is held together by its Windforest soul.

We must cultivate our minds and actions, but we can do it well only in terms of the Windforest of truths and minds and cultivated actions within which we are merely pockets of localized weather, but interconnected with all the climates that are. We must cultivate this Windforest with respect for its established ways of bringing fruitfulness about and with hospitality to its random gifts that puff us into the realization that who we are, both individually and together, *always* calls for revision, and that the shared Windforest of our minds somewhere and somehow provides what is needful to discern and accomplish what is to be cultivated next. The winds are full of wild yeasts that can both leaven and destroy. We must be both careful and adventurous, because we are far too unfinished to be safe from harm-doing—either suffering or perpetrating it—or beyond desirable (or even indispensable) improvement.

If our freedom means that there is little that we *must* do, including cultivating our illusorily *own* gardens, it also means that there is little that we *cannot* do. To raise our consciousness to this level of comprehensiveness and intimate awareness, and to keep it accessible as a guide in our doing and understanding, there is a practical way of directing our minds anywhere, anytime, briefly or sustainedly, always familiar and always new, inexhaustible and illuminating:

A Parting Word

The beginning of this book said that there were two Windforests. There are of course three. One is the book, which is now over, and has attempted to take you through the door to the second: the vast and intricate Windforest of the world's enduring life, its soul and mirror. The third is the Windforest that is peculiarly ours: the Windforest of the mind, mirror and metaphor of all that lives, and window to its reality. And it makes even a better door than a window. Walk its paths, and take care of what you find.

Windforest: take our breath away,
and return it to us refreshed with the life
you can give it.
Take it to the ends of the earth, to nourish what
you sustain,
and bring back what is offered you there to
sustain others.
Transform our breath so that new life can
be nurtured;
transform our minds and hearts in your image,
so that we can learn that we can give what we
do not own
and that we must be grateful for all that you touch
and quicken.
Windforest: spirit, soul of all that lives,
give as you have always given,
and show as you have always shown,
as we put our poor and priceless lives, all together,
into your keeping.

Let us cultivate our Windforest.

Ellen Fremedon

Ellen Fremedon has been a student of religion for as long as she can remember, and a practitioner even longer. A lifelong Catholic who grows steadily more grateful for being one as the years pass, she has also enjoyed the privilege of studying and worshipping with other Christian groups (Orthodox, Protestant, Mormon) and with non-Christians as well (Jewish, Buddhist, Hindu, Muslim). She studied the work of John Main with the late Bede Griffiths at Saccidananda in India, pursued Buddhist studies in Japan, did Catholic scriptural, historical, and dogmatic work with Jean Daniélou and colleagues in Paris, and has spent time in schools, conferences, and temples of varying kinds in many parts of the world. She currently lives in seclusion.

Windforest

Windforest is a book that was conceived in the course of meditative exercise, developed through meditation, and eventually written because that appeared to the author the proper way to be faithful to what she had received. It is an exploration of the world of living beings and of the corresponding world of wind and air in which life is situated and nourished. It is meant to guide the reader into thoughtful ways of contemplating, and to provide a new manner of perceiving the intricate world in which we, along with all else, live: a vivid and inescapable truth, yet elusive; a concrete reality, and at the same time a subtle metaphor . . . .